GUITAR LEGENDARY LICKS

METALLICA
1988-1996

Other Metallica Legendary Licks books available:

Metallica Legendary Licks Guitar 1983-1988 02500181
Metallica Legendary Licks Bass 02500180
Metallica Legendary Licks Drums 02500172

Recording Credits:
Doug Boduch, guitar
Tom McGir, bass
Scott Schroedl, drums
Jake Johnson, recording and mixing engineer
Todd Greene, producer

Cover photography by Ross Halfin/Idols

ISBN 1-57560-285-7

Visit our website at www.cherrylane.com

Photography by Anton Corbijn

Contents

Editor's Note: Tune guitars down one whole step (D G C F A D) for "Sad but True" and down one half step (E♭ A♭ D♭ G♭ B♭ E♭) for all songs from *Load* and *Reload*.

Introduction

The early 1980s: glam-rock predominated the loosely defined heavy metal genre. Rock groups with teased hair and make-up pumped out sugarcoated pop songs that filled the airwaves. It was in this unlikely state of affairs that a four-man aural assault called Metallica emerged from the San Francisco Bay Area and tore its way into music history. The group's conquest began in 1983 when their debut album, *Kill 'Em All,* sent a jolt into the ears of metal fans and critics alike and has continued, with ever-growing successes, to the present day.

As Metallica continues to break new ground and compound its own legend, there are no limits in sight. And now, with this book, there is no limit to what you can learn about how the guitar has contributed to that success.

Metallica Legendary Licks–Guitar 1983-1988 presents a comprehensive play-along package that includes note-for-note transcriptions and recordings. The transcriptions present every note, in tablature and standard notation, just as James Hetfield and Kirk Hammett played them. There are no vocals on the CD, so it's easy to hear exactly what the instruments are doing. You'll also find slowed-down versions of the fast and tricky passages, which make the learning process that much simpler. The detailed performance notes in the book will give you insightful perspectives on your favorite Metallica songs and help you play them even better. Further, the recording is split channel, so you can listen to all the instruments or play along with the band. In short, listen and learn—and you'll be thrashing and shredding in no time.

A Historical Retrospective of Metallica

. . . And Justice for All (1988)

It is probably not accidental that green and black were chosen for *. . . And Justice for All's* cover art, for its title track deals with the evils (black) of money (green) while "Blackened" speaks of the end (black) of the earth (green). *. . . And Justice for All* marked a first and a last for Metallica: it was the first album with Jason Newsted on bass (following Cliff Burton's tragic death) and the last of Metallica's collaborations with long-time producer Flemming Rasmussen. This unique album will be remembered as Metallica's most extreme venture into the world of musical complexity. Pounding power chords (made to sound even thicker by multi-track layering), galloping palm-muted bass notes, and vicious rhythmic accents played by the whole band are aspects of Metallica's bone-crushing delivery, heard throughout the long and complex song forms found on *. . . And Justice for All.*

Metallica (1991)

Perhaps in direct response to the slightly esoteric musical complexity of *. . . And Justice for All, Metallica* was the group's most accessible album to date and caught the ears of many new listeners who had never enjoyed Metallica's music before. Its more traditional arrangements and "radio-friendly" production still captured the aggression that had earned Metallica its headbanging loyalists, but was now better suited for MTV and other mass outlets. Surely the biggest catalyst in these changes was the designation of Bob Rock as producer for the album. Rock had a distinct influence on many aspects of Metallica's sound, from production methods to stylistic choices. Take note of the many clean guitar parts used throughout, including solo and fingerstyle passages. Everything you would expect from musicians that have traveled around the world—from exotic modes, such as Phrygian, to the electric sitar (used in "Wherever I May Roam")—is heard on this album.

Load (1996)

Load clearly demonstrated that the group had continued to grow musically in the five years since *Metallica.* One of the album's many assets was bringing the musical voices of Kirk Hammett and Jason Newsted to the foreground. A second was the group's decision to, for the first time, record the drum and bass tracks prior to the other tracks, which would establish a tight rhythmic foundation upon which the remaining instruments could build. Though *Metallica* had planted the seeds for change in the group's style, it was *Load* and the subsequent *Reload* that brought about a feeling of unlimited new potential among the members of Metallica.

Reload (1997)

Reload is essentially a continuation of *Load*, as all of the songs were written during the same period of great inspiration that led up to *Load*. Deadlines for the completion of Load's recording, coupled with the abundance of worthy material, led to a decision in January 1996 to divide the songs into two equally strong batches and release the second as a separate, follow-up album in 1997.

Where will Metallica go next? Regardless of the answer, one can trust that the essential qualities that have been the hallmarks of their remarkable success—honest delivery, rigorous self-improvement, and the drive for artistic innovation, to name just a few—will continue to thrill their millions of devoted fans.

When Two Become One: Creative Arranging Using Twin-Guitar Harmonies

Among the many factors contributing to Metallica's continued success is their ability to consistently maintain a fresh sound. This is the result not only of their sheer songwriting prowess, but also of the crafty arranging of their guitar parts. Typically most two-guitar bands have the roles of each guitarist clearly delineated, with one guitarist relegated to the role of rhythm guitarist and the other designated as the lead, and both guitarists playing the same rhythm part when the singer is singing or doubling a riff in unison. Metallica is no exception, and certainly a large portion of their songs have James chording and Kirk wailing. But Metallica also knows how to make full use of the textural possibilities offered by having two guitarists.

The twin-guitar harmonized melody is one of Metallica's most distinctive arranging trademarks. This texture, popularized by Iron Maiden, takes full advantage of a two-guitar band situation, allowing each guitarist an equal share of the spotlight and providing the listener with textural contrast.

Arranging a harmony part for a second guitar is relatively simple, once you understand the mechanics, and will provide a thorough lesson in fretboard mechanics. Let's examine some of Metallica's examples.

The wistful melody in the interlude of "Nothing Else Matters" is harmonized in 3rds or 4ths. This simply means that both guitars mimic each others melodic movement and are always separated by a 3rd (three scale steps) or a 4th (four scale steps). Play through each of the guitar parts separately and observe the similarities in shape and contour of each part.

*Gtr. II notated to left of slashes.

A melody can be harmonized using any interval between the two guitars. Riff B from "The Unforgiven II" is harmonized in 6ths.

Gtr. II to left of slash.

The first step in creating twin-guitar, harmonized melodies is to find the starting note for each guitar. The interval between these notes determine the effect produced and, as a general rule, 3rds and 6ths are the most harmonious, and 2nds and 7ths are the most discordant. Once you find the starting note for each guitar's part, then simply let the two guitars shadow each other's melodic motion, using only the notes from the scale source for diatonic (in key) harmonizations and employing the appropriate non-scale notes for chromatic (notes that are not in the key) harmonizations.

Tone Clone: How To Replicate The Metallica Guitar Sound

To achieve a guitar tone similar to Metallica's using a basic setup, the key is in the settings. Select the bridge pickup (preferably a humbucker) on your guitar and turn the tone and volume knobs all the way up. The distortion, whether derived from your amp's lead channel or a distortion pedal should be set with the gain at the maximum level, to allow for total saturation. Use an EQ pedal or the tone knobs on your amp to boost the highs and lows while cutting down on the mids. Doing this keeps the sound from getting muddy, which is the natural tendency as more distortion is added, and allows the notes to cut through clearly.

Gear Setups

James Hetfield

On stage, James Hetfield uses either a Mesa Boogie 4 x 12 (four 12-inch speakers) cabinet with Vintage 30 Speakers or a Wizard 4 x 12, with 25-watt Greenbacks. With his Juice Goose power strip, Hetfield fires up two Sony WRR-840 wireless systems and a TC Electronics M2000 effects processor. Also housed in the amp rack are two Mesa Boogie Graphic EQs (custom) and two Mesa Boogie Strategy 400 power amps. Stomp boxes include a MXR Phase 100, Cry Baby or Vox wah-wah pedal, Digitech whammy pedal, Brown Source distortion, ElectroHarmonix bass synthesizer, and a stereo chorus pedal.

Hetfield owns many ESP custom guitars, usually loaded with EMG pickups. Besides the steel string acoustic and nylon string guitars, Hetfield owns a Ken Lawrence Custom Explorer (natural) and two National Resophonic Reso-Electrics (one black and one tobacco). He also uses a Fender Telecaster that has the famed Parsons/White string bender for the "The Unforgiven II."

All the electric guitars are strung up with Ernie Ball Regular Slinky (.010–.046 gauge) and the pick of choice is a Dunlop Custom Nylon.

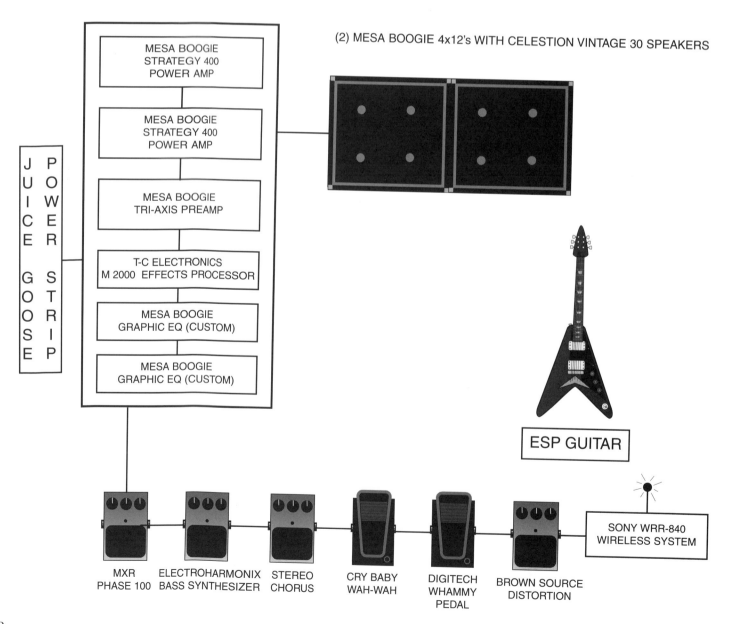

Kirk Hammett

For live performance, Hammett uses Marshall 4 x 12 cabinets with 25 watt speakers and Mesa/Boogie Strategy 400 power amps. Bradshaw preamps and VHT power amps are also used. In the studio, Hammett prefers to go with a Boogie Mark IV head, ADA MP-1 preamp, Vintage Marshall head, and Mesa/Boogie 4 x 12 cabinets with 25-watt speakers. Hammett's effects include an Eventide H3000, a Boss SE-50, an Ibanez Tube Screamer, an Aphex parametric EQ (studio), a stereo chorus, a Cry Baby wah-wah, and some vintage effect pedals (Electro-Harmonix, MXR, etc.).

Like Hetfield, Kirk Hammett owns many ESP guitars loaded with EMG pickups. Other guitars include a Jackson Randy Rhoads Custom (tuned down a whole step), a 1958 Gibson Flying V (studio guitar), a Tom Anderson guitar (studio guitar), a Les Paul Custom, a Les Paul Standard (studio guitar), and early '60s Fender Strats, also for recording. Unlike Hetfield, Hammett uses Dean Markley strings (.010–.046 gauge) and a Dunlop green tortex pick.

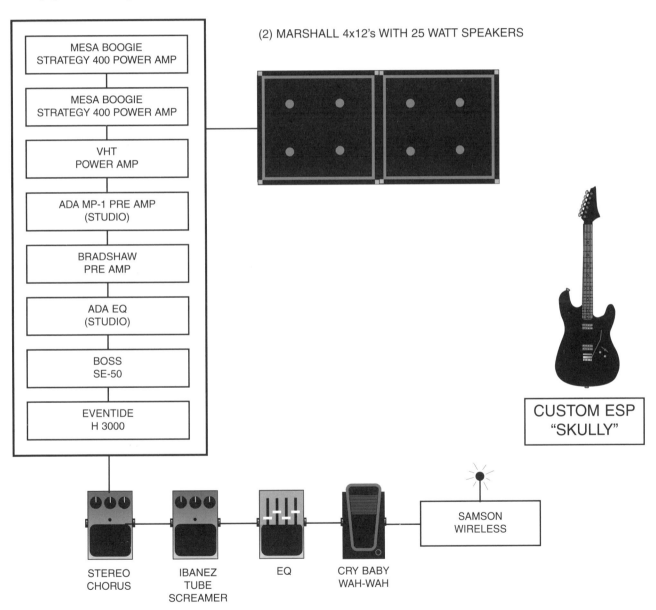

All of this information will help you get started emulating some of the sounds from Metallica, but remember not to be a slave to your equipment. Make the equipment work for you. If you know the guitar well and you have a sound in your head, then turning to electronics and gear is the right move; but if you jump into all this hi-tech stuff first without being able to play, then spend more time in the practice room and less time in the music store, otherwise you're not only being untrue to yourself, but your voice may get lost in all those effects and patch cords. Good luck!

About the Author

Guitarist and teacher, Nick Russo lives in New York and earned a M.A. in jazz performance from the Aaron Copland School of Music at Queens College, under the direction of Jimmy Heath, Sir Roland Hanna, and Tony Purrone. Private study with the legendary master, Billy Bauer, Tony Purrone, Dr. Steve Salerno, and Dr. David Belser has led to a life of full-time performing, including performances at Lincoln Center and the Knitting Factory in New York City, and Huis Ten Bosch in Sasebo, Japan. In addition to performing with Teddy Charles, Sonny Dallas, Todd Coolman, Jim Nolet, Tony Moreno, Elliot Zigmund, Mike Hall, Joe Ascione, and John Ray, Nick Russo has recorded with Sonny Dallas, Jim Nolet, Tony Moreno, and Tim Berne.

Nick Russo

Acknowledgments

I want to thank the following people for their support; my parents, Nancy and Rich Russo; Stan Young; Alec Petkoff; Kim Cavallo; Lisa (Ivy) Hochberg; Arthur Rotfeld; Joe Charupakorn; and especially Nancy (Nai Hua) Liu.

One

from . . . And Justice for All

Words and Music by
James Hetfield and Lars Ulrich

This is a quintessential Metallica tune and a great starter for beginning guitarists. The opening figure (Rhy. Fig.1) is simple yet fun to play, and the guitar solo in the intro is melodic and manageable even for novices.

Intro

The opening rhythm guitar part outlines Bm (B D F♯), Gmaj7 (G B D F♯), and D (D F♯ A). Notice how the open D string acts as a unifying thread between these chords. Also, do you hear the striking similarity between "Fade to Black" (see *Metallica Legendary Licks, 1983-1988*) and "One"?

Hammett uses the B natural minor scale (B C♯ D E F♯ G A) and the B minor arpeggio (B D F♯) in his solo. Remember the A–B motive in "Fade to Black"? Well, check out bars 4–7 of the introduction's guitar solo in "One."

The B minor arpeggio at the beginning of the 2nd phrase (when the drums enter) can best be executed using sweep picking, a technique where you *sweep* across several strings in one direction with the pick, minimizing right-hand motion. Sweep picking is easiest if you tilt the pick and "brush" the strings gently without digging in too much. In other words, don't put too much pick in between the strings.

After the guitar solo, Hetfield varies the dark, B minor opening figure with a more promising riff in the relative major key of D (Riff A).

TRACK 01

Full Band

TRACK 02

Slow Demo (Gtr. II)

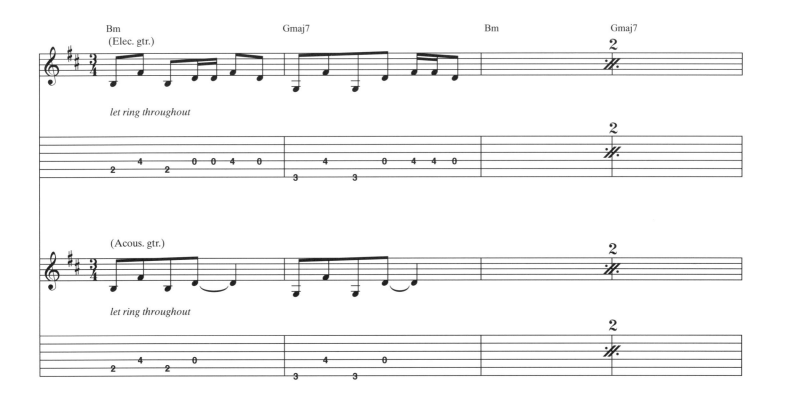

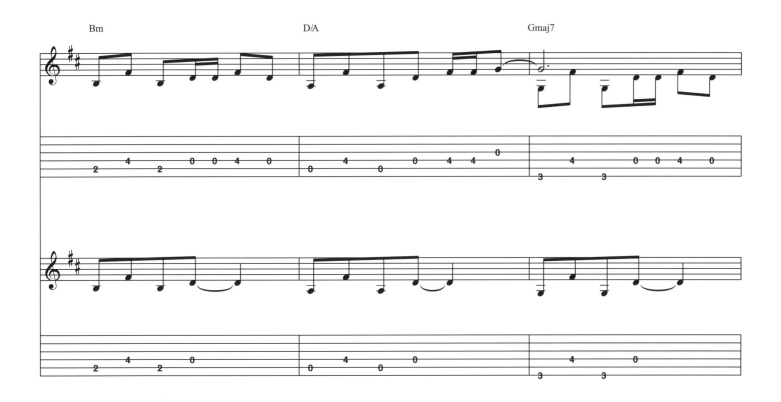

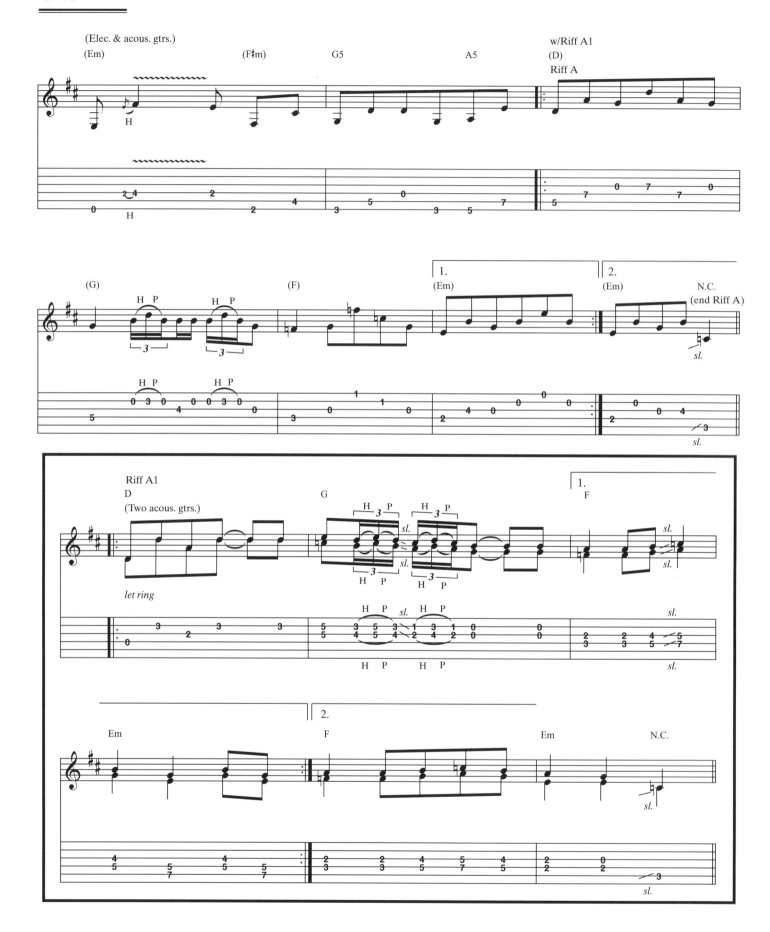

Solo

The second phrase of this catchy solo is a repeat of the first, just an octave higher. The ending gets altered slightly, as triplets are spun out of the three-note descending pattern that Hammett uses so often. Tap using the edge of the pick while keeping the left-hand fingers on the other two notes. The aftermath of the tap should sound the second note, while the pull-off should sound the third note of the triplet.

TRACK 03
Full Band

TRACK 04
Slow Demo

*Tap using edge of pick. *Silent taps.

Sixteenth-Note Triplet Riff

Every rock drummer wanted a double bass drum pedal when this song first came out and, undoubtedly, every guitarist should learn this badass sixteenth-note triplet riff. F5 adds some ♭2 horror to this already shocking rhythm as Hetfield sings "Darkness imprisoning me . . ."

TRACK 05

Full Band

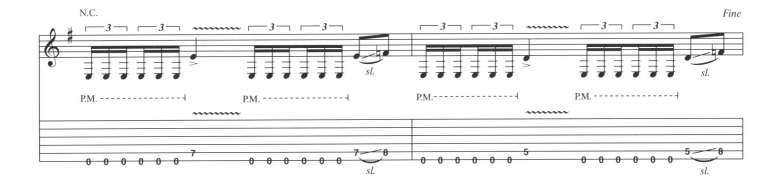

Main Solo

This solo is obviously a development of the triplet ideas from the previous section, arpeggiating Em, C, Bm, G, Am, and F triads, all superimposed over E5 and F5 chords! The three-note, descending pattern (B–A–G) in bars 16–17 is an expansion of bar 8 from the earlier solo. Although this may have been an improvised solo, some things were worked out in advance, such as the band locking in with Hammett's double-stop bends in bars 27–28 and 31–32.

Full Band   Slow Demo

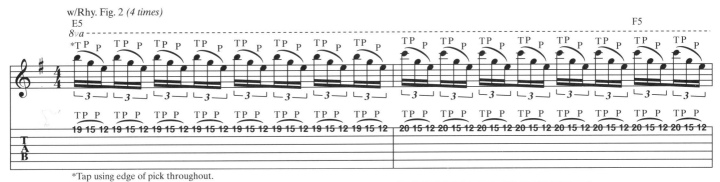

*Tap using edge of pick throughout.

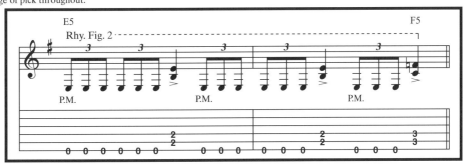

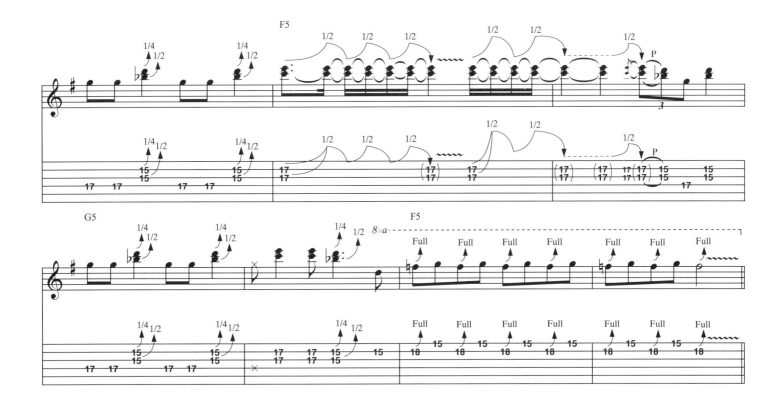

The Shortest Straw

from *. . . And Justice for All*

Words and Music by
James Hetfield and Lars Ulrich

This is a classic heavy metal march that contains an absolutely amazing guitar solo, perhaps Hammett's best—replete with an encyclopedia of guitar techniques, including ear-splitting harmonics, ultra-wide tremolo bar work, and fiery arpeggios.

Solo

Hammett took ten lessons from Joe Satriani right before *Kill 'Em All* was recorded, and although Satriani's influence can be heard in earlier solos, it is most apparent in this selection, with its hairy tremolo work, use of harmonics, and lightning-fast, arpeggiated pull-offs. Notice how Hammett reverts back to the older, bluesier style only in bars 5, 6, and 12 with the E blues scale (E G A B♭ B D) and E Dorian mode (E F♯ G A B C♯ D). The Pat Metheny–esque lick in bars 13 and 14 is played by moving dyads (two-note chords) down the fingerboard chromatically on the G and D strings. Don't miss the "outside" (notes not in the key) effect he gets by alternating two triads (E major and B♭ major) a tritone apart in bar 15. Don't let the challenging pull-offs in bars 17–20 intimidate you: these are just arpeggios outlining the chords notated above the staff (F♯, G, E/G♯, and A). These arpeggios all have the same fingering pattern except for E/G♯, which requires a bit more stretching because it's in first inversion, with the G♯ as the lowest note.

TRACK 08
Full Band

TRACK 09
Slow Demo

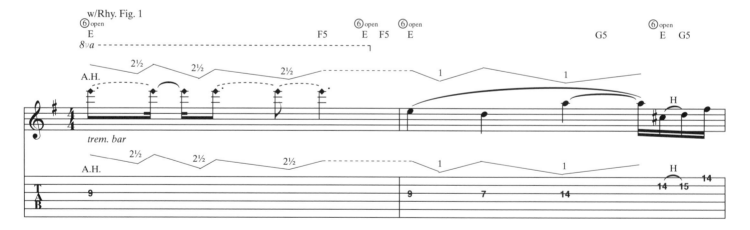

23

The Shortest Straw *Cont.*

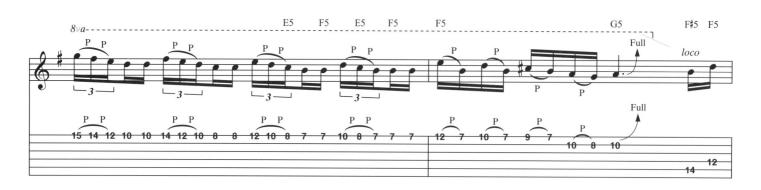

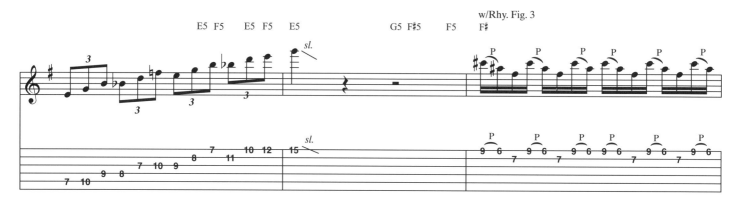

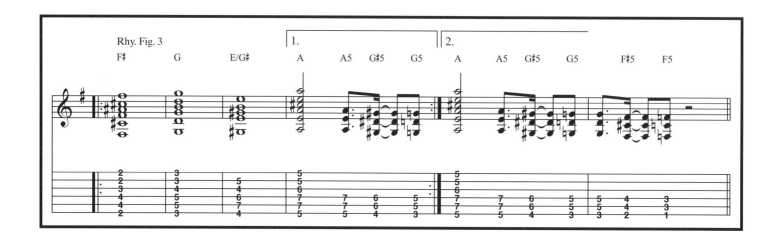

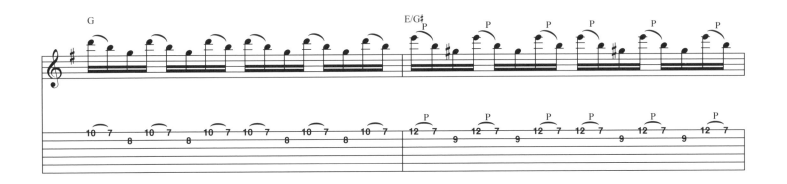

Enter Sandman

from *Metallica*

Words and Music by
James Hetfield, Lars Ulrich and Kirk Hammett

Don't pass this one up . . . beginners can handle the rhythm guitar parts, while advanced players can take on the solo. "Enter Sandman" is not only one of Metallica's most popular songs, but it also offers something for every guitarist to learn.

Intro

Feelings of anticipation permeate this intro, as the Em ostinato figure summons the other guitar parts. Gtr. II enters with an Em chord, played through a wah pedal, and followed by a more driving version of the ostinato (Gtr. III), which enters in eighth notes while Gtr. IV sustains the E5 power chord. To keep us on the edge of our seat, Gtr. III is then infected with the trademark intervals $\flat$5 (B$\flat$) and $\flat$2 (F) on the "ands" of beats 2 and 4. More embellishments are added until finally, the full-fledged Rhy. Fig. 2 breaks in, with F$\sharp$5 and G5 as its tail!

TRACK 10

Full Band

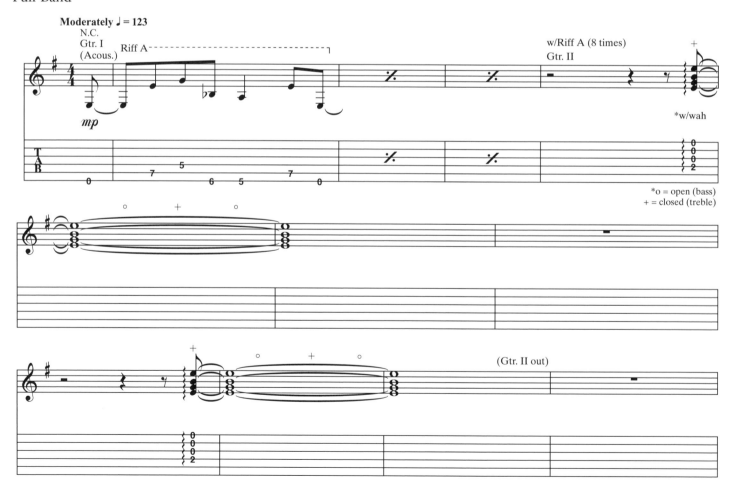

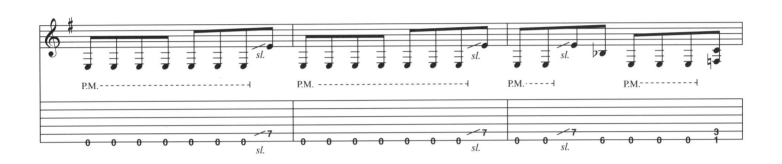

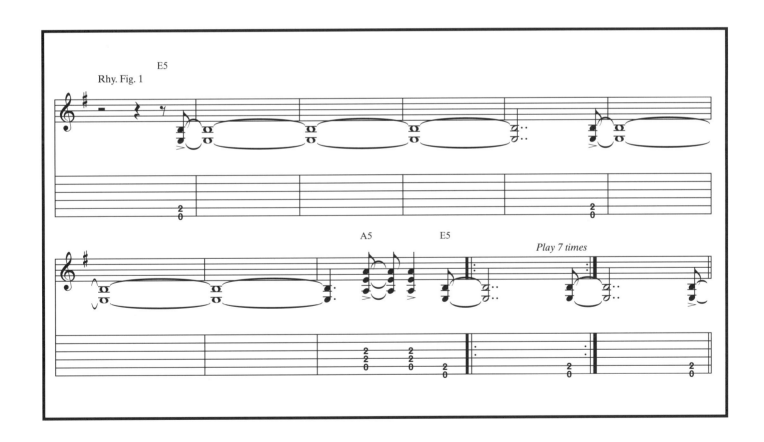

Enter Sandman Cont.

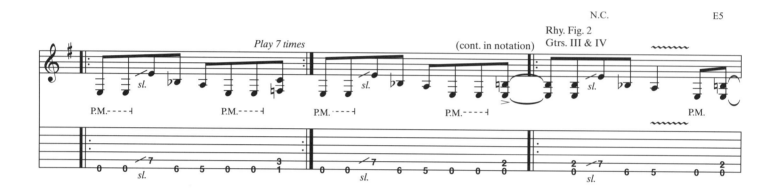

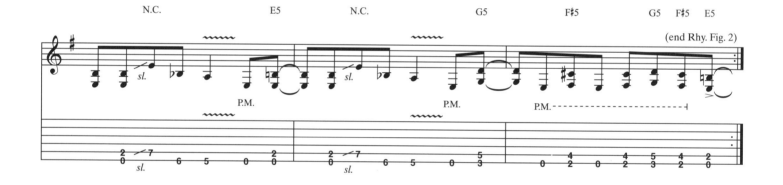

Pre-Chorus and Chorus Riff

A brief modulation up a whole step heightens the tension as Rhy. Fig. 2 is now reiterated in F# minor (Rhy. Fig. 3). The half time feel throws us off balance, making us expect the unexpected. The chorus throws us back into the original time/feel as Rhy. Fig. 4 delivers a heavier version of the original ostinato.

TRACK 11

Full Band

Solo

Hammett uses wah-driven blues licks from the E pentatonic minor scale (E G A B D) to start his improvisation. The arpeggios in bars 7 and 8 are simply diatonic triads found in the E Dorian mode. D major and E minor are deployed in bar 7 while A major comes in the first half of bar 8. At the modulation, Hammett is bending 3rds in a bluesy manner until he evokes the F♯ Phrygian mode (F♯ G A B C♯ D E) in bar 11. After the blues lick from bar 13 is handsomely developed, the A major arpeggio returns, this time superimposed over F♯m producing an F♯m7 (F♯ A C♯ E) sound. E Dorian makes another appearance in the last five bars, with a strong presence of the sustained C♯ or 6th (the 6th degree, in combination with the flatted 3rd, gives Dorian its character).

TRACK 12
Full Band

TRACK 13
Slow Demo

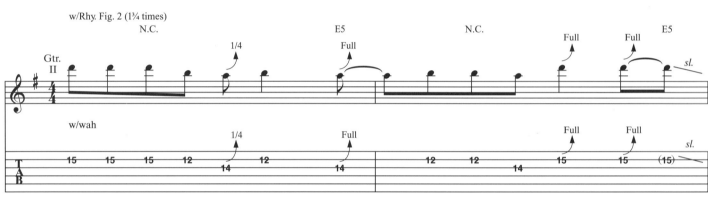

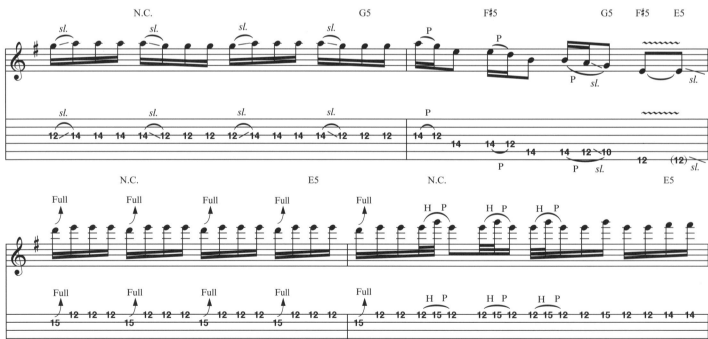

Solo

We're still in Hammett's bluesy period, as this solo clearly exhibits. More dirty double-stops bends, pentatonic minor scales, blue notes (in the form of microtones reached by bending the strings), and the Mixolydian mode. In bar 7, Hammett toggles between the A Mixolydian mode (A B C♯ D E F♯ G) and the A Dorian mode (A B C D E F♯ G) with a sequential, sextuplet lick in the style of Steve Vai. A darker mood is evoked in the last three bars, as the F♯'s are replaced with F♮'s, eliciting a change from A Dorian to A natural minor (A B C D E F G).

TRACK 19
Full Band

TRACK 20
Slow Demo

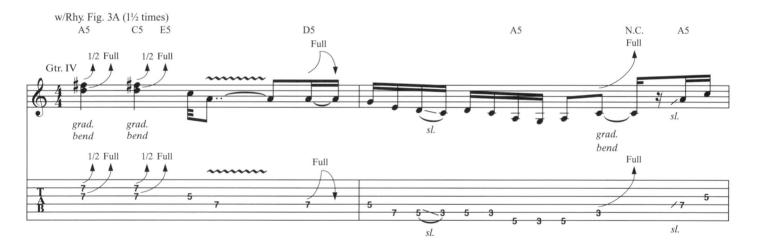

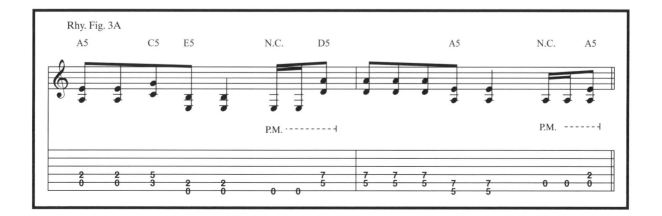

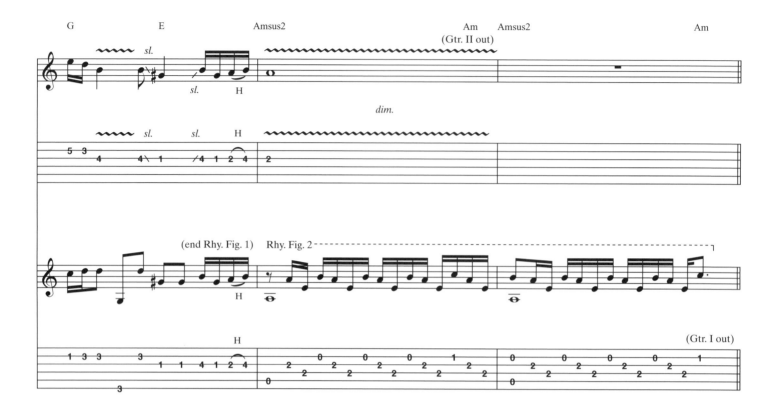

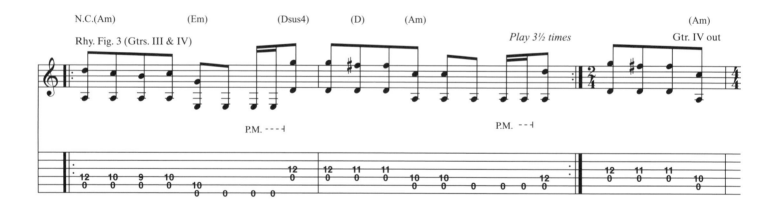

The Unforgiven Cont.

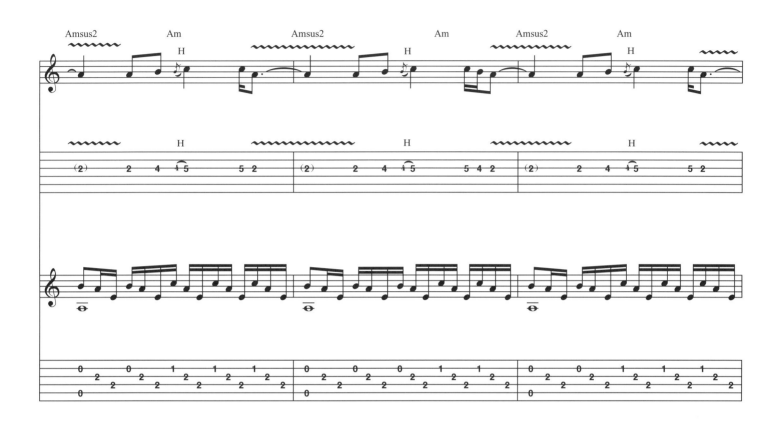

The Unforgiven

from *Metallica*

Words and Music by
James Hetfield, Lars Ulrich and Kirk Hammett

The opening acoustic guitar part requires fingerstyle technique, whereas the verse riff (Rhy. Fig. 3) and solo can be performed with a pick.

Opening and Verse

The ubiquitous bell toll heard here made its inaugural appearance in "For Whom the Bell Tolls," but also sets an ominous tone for this song. To play the Amsus2 (A B E) chord in Gtr. I, use *p* (thumb) for the sustaining, open A string, and memorize a right-hand finger pattern for *i* (index), *m* (middle), and *a* (ring). One suggestion is: *a m i, a m i a, m i a m, i a m i.*

Hetfield teases us by first playing only three notes, then giving us the complete phrase as the bass enters in bar 10. Rhy. Fig. 1 outlines the chord progression for this phrase (Amsus2–C–G–Em–Amsus2–C–G–E). Use *p* for the lowest notes and alternate with *i*, *m*, and *a* for the higher strings, respectively.

Rhy. Fig. 3 (Gtrs. III & IV), from the verse, is a guitar part that stands on its own. The part mimics the vocal line, with single notes on open-string pedals to provide support. Take note of the chords, notated above the staff, that are implied in the intervals formed by the open strings and fretted notes. Gtr. III continues alone with a sixteenth-note riff that has palm-muted (P.M.) open A and open D strings embedded within a stepwise, descending, A minor melody.

TRACK 18

Full Band

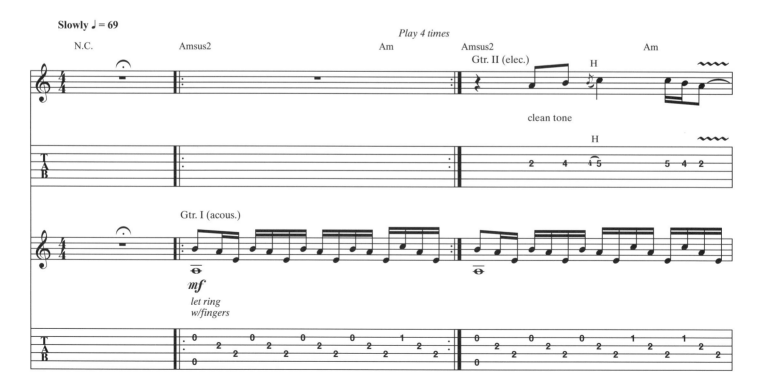

Sad but True Cont.

Sad but True

from *Metallica*

Words and Music by James
Hetfield and Lars Ulrich

Help yourself to another heaping of Metallica's slow heaviness. Blues lovers will find pleasure in the killin' groove heard during the intro and the solo. The bridge from blues to heavy metal can be found in the chorus riff, with the addition of ♭II and ♭V chords.

Intro: Spacious Entrance and Killin' Groove

Tuned down a whole step, Hetfield is sustaining A and B♭ chords to create suspense for the upcoming killin' groove. Leaving space (either by sustaining notes or using rests) allows the music to breathe, and leaves the listener in anticipation for the next event. The 5 1/2 beats of complete silence is very effective.

The heavy, E blues groove that follows is unusual for Metallica in that they are not using any ♭II or ♭V, chords—it sounds like Chicago blues gone metal!

TRACK 14

Full Band

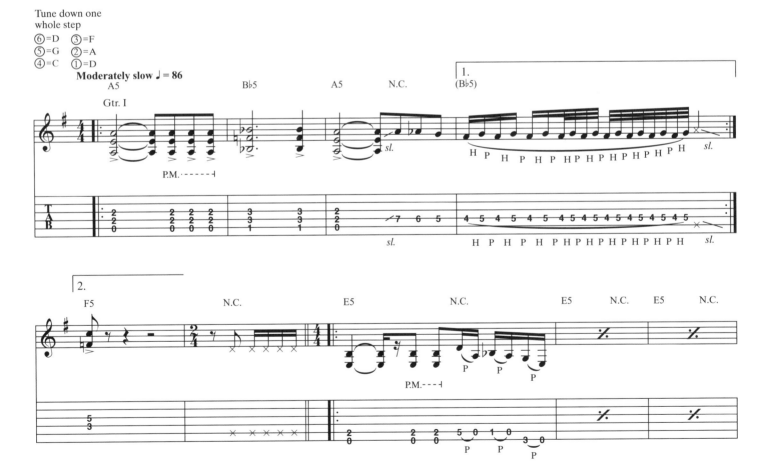

Enter Sandman Cont.

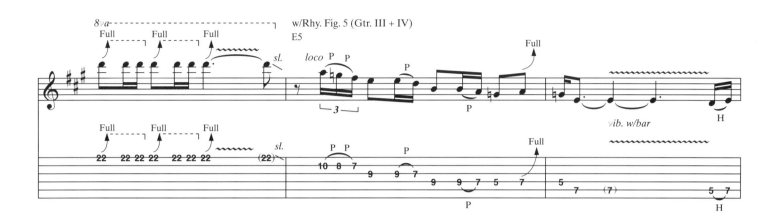

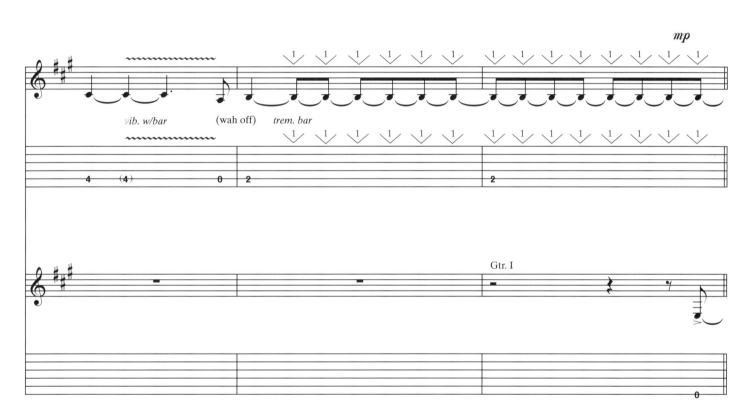

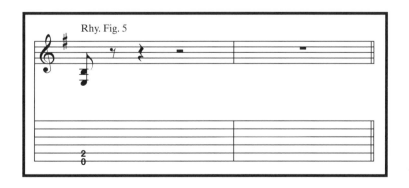

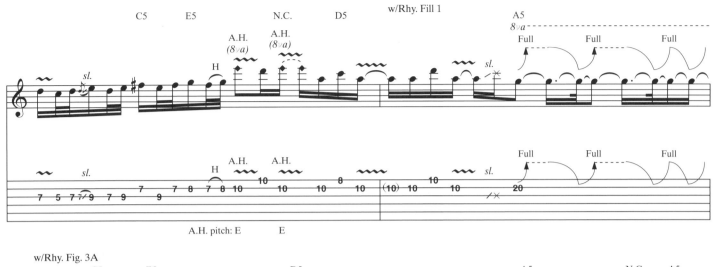

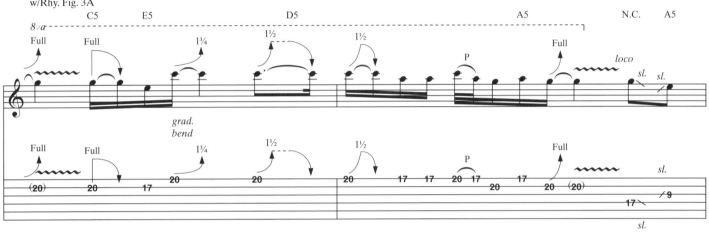

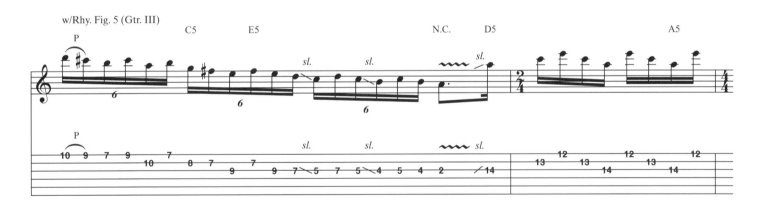

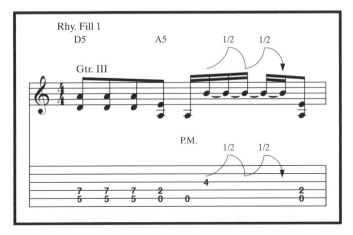

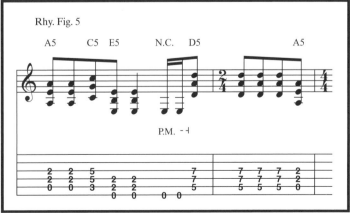

The Unforgiven Cont.

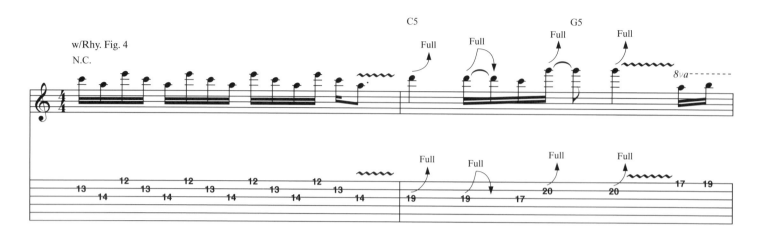

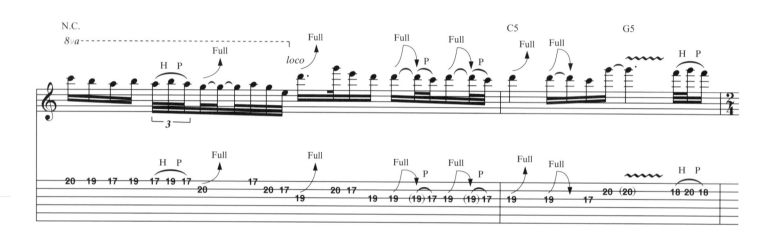

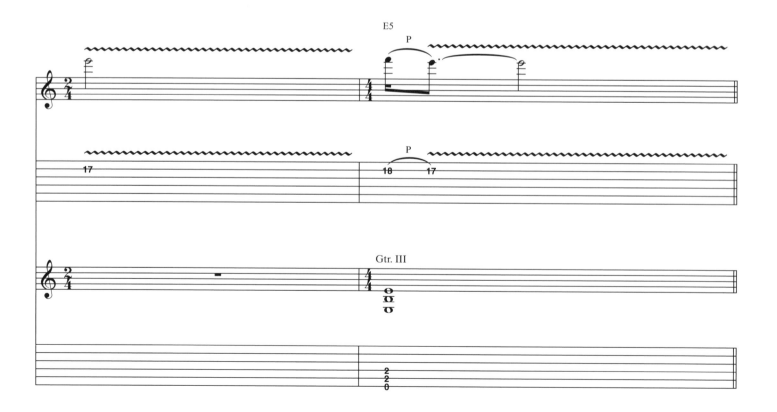

Nothing Else Matters

from *Metallica*

Words and Music by
James Hetfield and Lars Ulrich

Solo guitar connoisseurs will appreciate the opening, while lovers of clean guitar tone will enjoy the interlude. Metallica again shows off their never-ending palette of guitar sounds. Beginning lead players should try the guitar solo because it is slow, melodic, and uses primarily one scale.

Opening

Every Metallica album has a few songs that start with an acoustic or clean guitar; this type of arrangement makes the entrance of the distorted guitar more effective, and provides contrast to the heavier songs.

Solo guitar can sometimes give the illusion of two or more parts played simultaneously, as seen in this example. A pattern of *p i m a m i* in the right hand will work for bars 1–3 and 13–15. Variations on this finger pattern may be used in other bars, but always observe the principle of alternating fingers—in other words, do not play two *i*'s, *m*'s or *a*'s in a row.

TRACK 21

Full Band

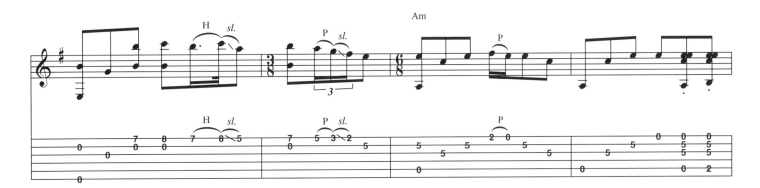

Nothing Else Matters Cont.

*Vol. knob swell.

Interlude (Clean Guitar Solo)

Grab another guitarist and work on this duet together. A well-written outgrowth of the opening, this interlude has a delicate blend of harmony, texture, and rhythm. As in most Metallica interludes, the second guitar provides an upper-harmony to thicken the texture.

Full Band

*Gtr. II notated to left of slashes.

Wherever I May Roam Cont.

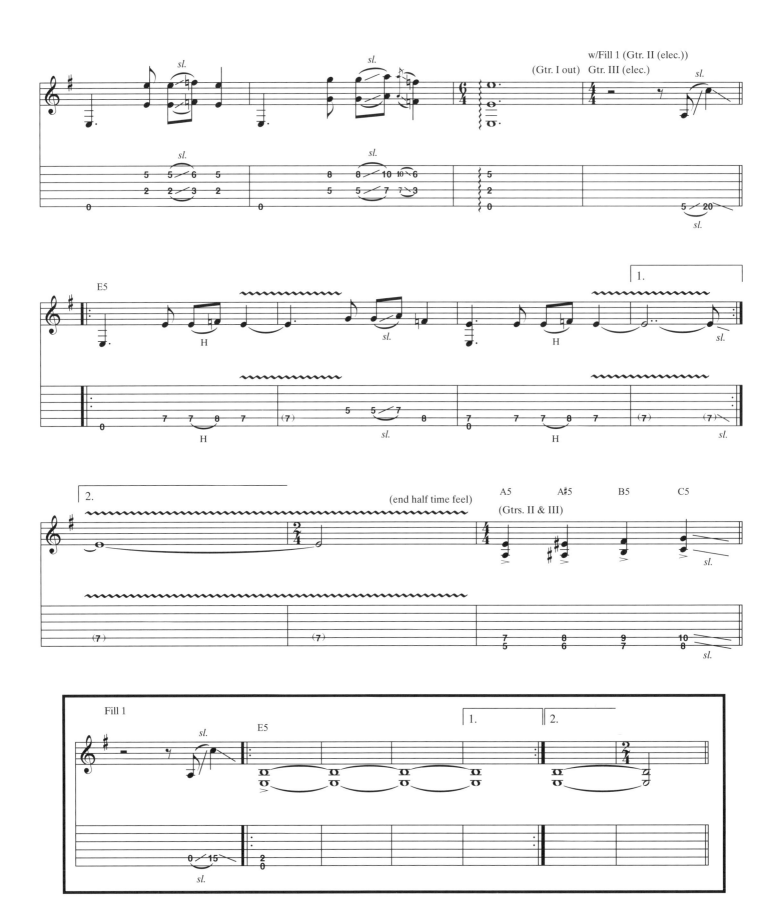

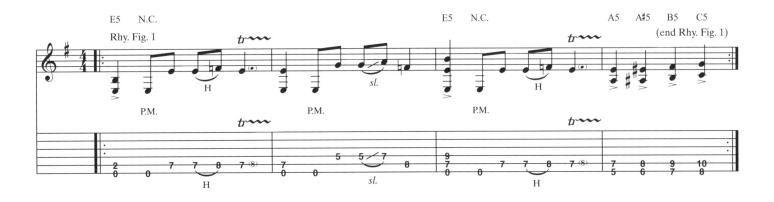

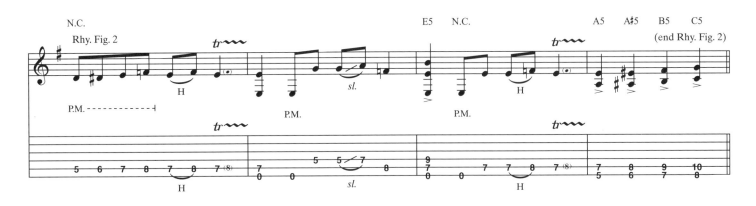

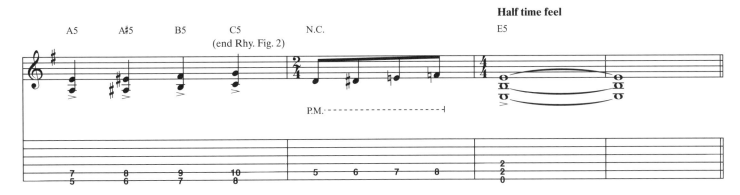

2 x 4

from *Load*

Words and Music by
James Hetfield, Lars Ulrich and Kirk Hammett

Copyright © 1996 Creeping Death Music (ASCAP)
International Copyright Secured All Rights Reserved

Tune your guitar down a half-step and get ready to shuffle! The shuffle, or triplet feel, could have been written in ¹²⁄₈, but with the (♫ = ♩♪) marking, we can easily read this in ⁴⁄₄.

Intro

This bluesy number contains galloping eighths like those found in "The Four Horsemen" *(Metallica Legendary Licks, Vol. 1)*. Shuffle eighths are eighth notes that are executed as the first two-thirds and the last third of an eighth-note triplet.

The notes in Riff A are from the E blues scale and emphasize ♭5, giving the riff its malignant quality. Riff B is a variation that incorporates the wah pedal and a quarter-step bent minor 3rd, but this time the triplet on beat 3 climbs up to an E, instead of B♭.

TRACK 26

Full Band

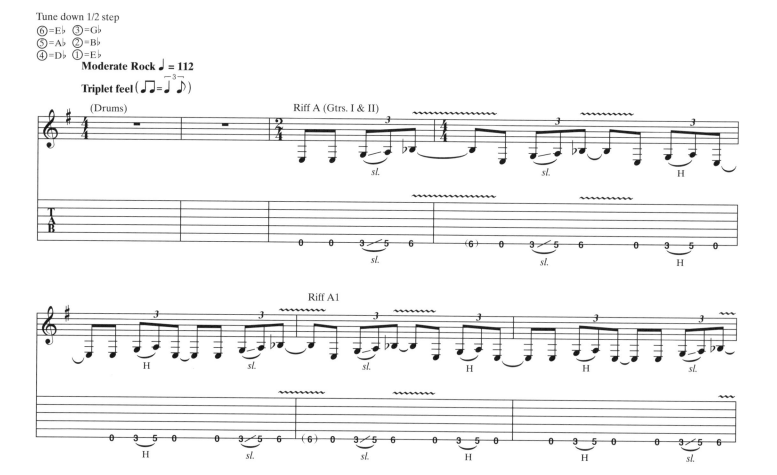

Until It Sleeps

from *Load*

Words and Music by
James Hetfield and Lars Ulrich

Get your feet wet with this tune. The verse riff is really easy and cool, and the chorus is very manageable.

Verse and Chorus

Call-and-response is another musical device found in many Metallica tunes. In this case, there is a call-and-response effect between the vocals and guitar (in Rhy. Fig. 1). At the chorus, Rhy. Fig. 2 dresses up Rhy. Fig. 1 with some 3rds, 4ths, open A string pedals and rhythmic variations. Prepare the fingers for the dyads so as not to block the sound of the palm-muted (P.M.) open A string.

TRACK 27

Full Band

Tune down 1/2 step
⑥=E♭ ③=G♭
⑤=A♭ ②=B♭
④=D♭ ①=E♭

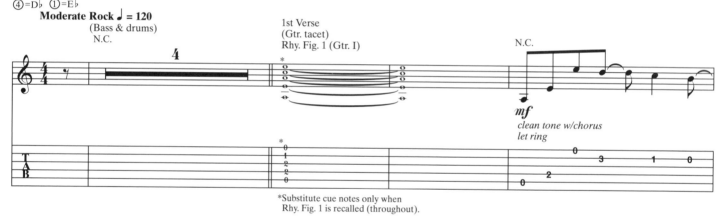

*Substitute cue notes only when
Rhy. Fig. 1 is recalled (throughout).

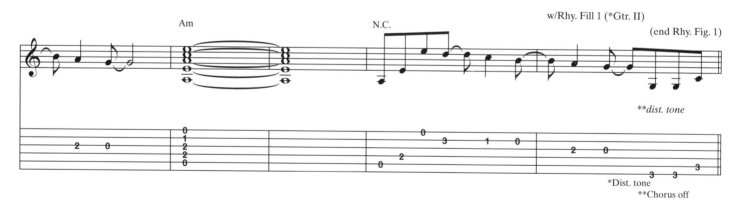

w/Rhy. Fig. 2A (4 times)

*Throughout Choruses, chord names indicated by Gtr. I.

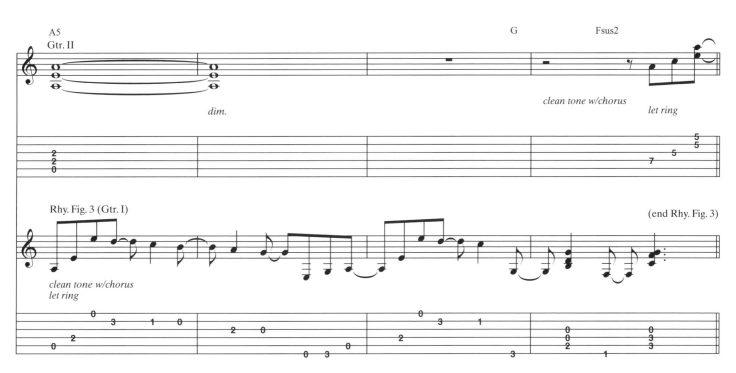

Solo

"The tritone is king!," as Hammett boldly juggles bends three half steps apart, evoking the solo melodies of the late Randy Rhoads. In bars 5–8, Hammett makes use of the open E string to create a catchy, rhythmic hook that leads to the contrasting, lyrical passage in a half time feel. After the half time feel, as if provoked, Hammett explodes into a series of wah-infested blues runs.

TRACK 31
Full Band

TRACK 32
Slow Demo

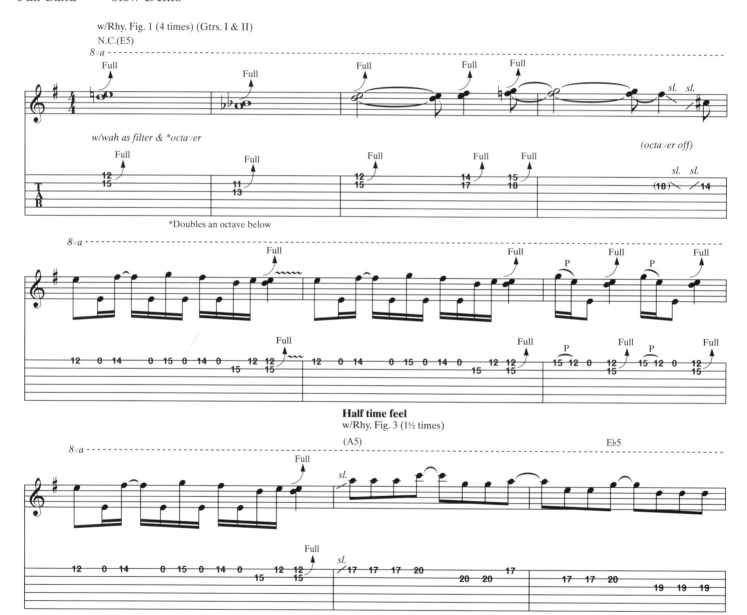

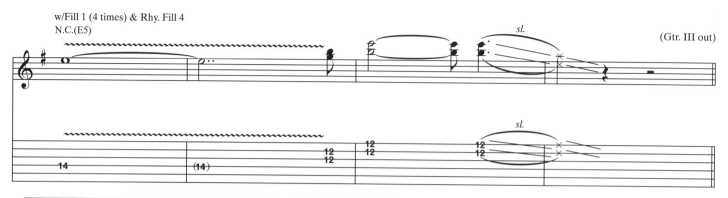

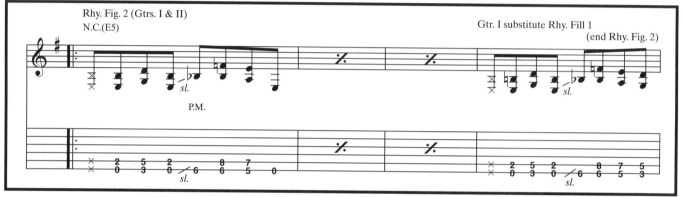

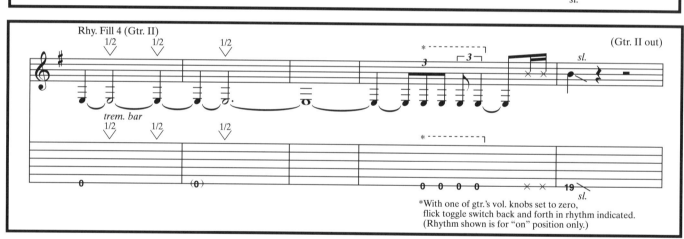

*With one of gtr.'s vol. knobs set to zero,
flick toggle switch back and forth in rhythm indicated.
(Rhythm shown is for "on" position only.)

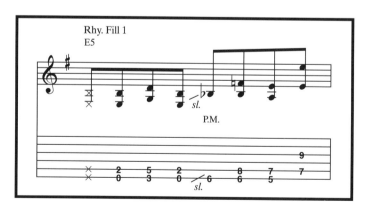

Hero of the Day

from *Load*

Words and Music by
James Hetfield, Lars Ulrich and Kirk Hammett

Metallica goes major! This is one of Metallica's only joyous, major-sounding intros. The riff is fairly easy and provides a good lesson in fretboard harmony.

Intro Riff

This intro is a good example of oblique motion (a contrapuntal technique in which one voice moves against a stationary line). Observe how, as the lower voice climbs up the A major scale (A B C♯ D E F♯ G♯), from A to E, the upper voices are static, until the E major chord in bars 3–4.

TRACK 33

Full Band

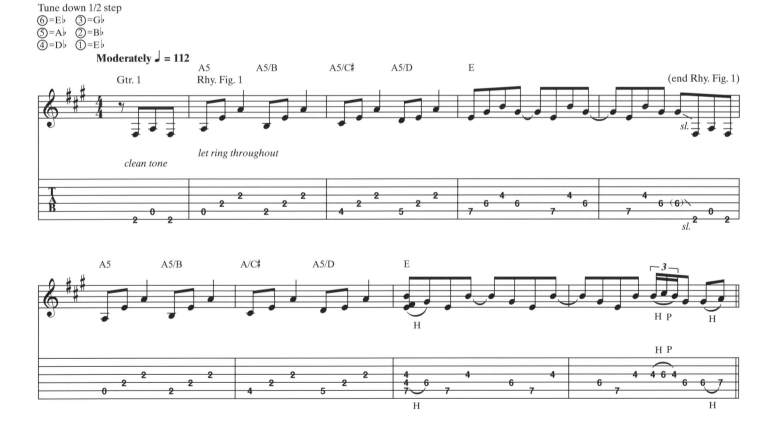

Fuel

from *Reload*

Words and Music by
James Hetfield, Lars Ulrich and Kirk Hammett

A strong blues flavor is evident here in both the riffs and the solo of "Fuel." Even the move to the IV chord (A) in a half time feel (in the intro) hints at a blues progression. Classic Metallica returns with the harmonized guitar part of the interlude.

Intro

You'll notice a *hemiola* (a *hemiola* occurs when notes or beats are repetitively phrased in an unusual grouping, creating an independent time/feel against the regular pulse) embedded in this riff. The eighths are grouped in a 3+3+2 pattern against an even, $\frac{4}{4}$ beat.

The move to the IV chord, A5, at the half time feel hints at a standard blues progression in E. The bends in this riff, as with all bends on the lower three strings, should be bent toward the higher strings (that is, toward the floor).

TRACK 34

Full Band

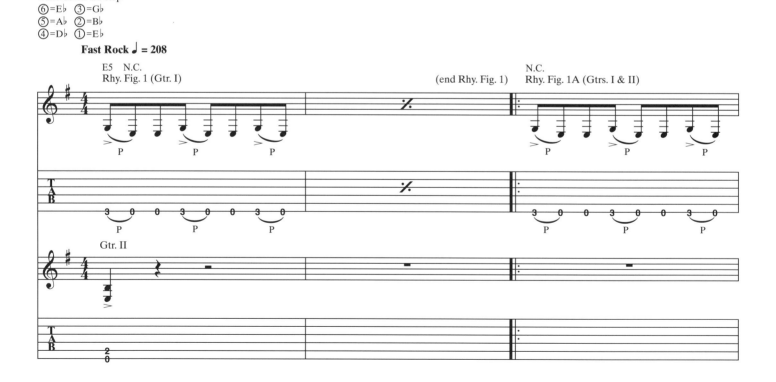

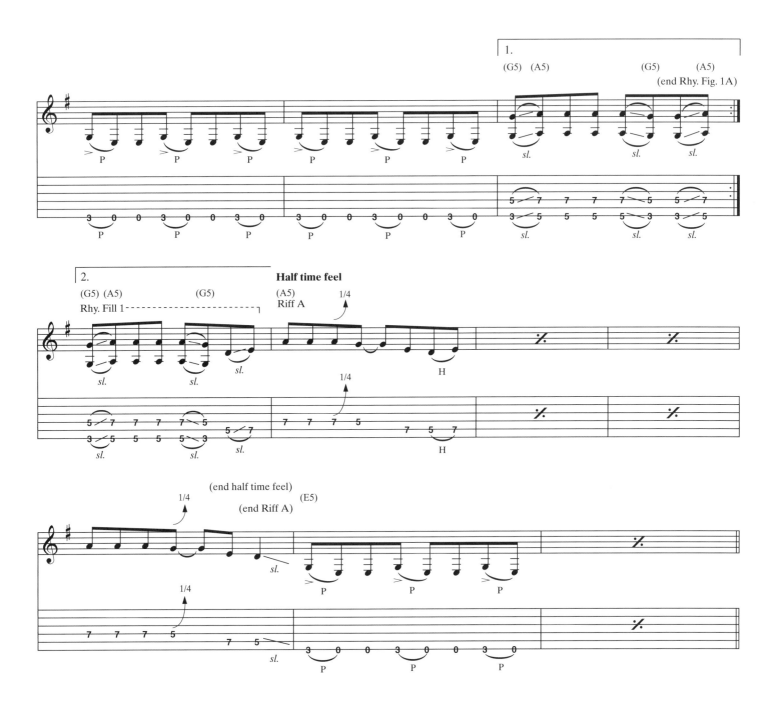

Interlude

The interlude is based on an E pentatonic minor figure (derived from Riff A in the intro) harmonized in 4ths.

Full Band

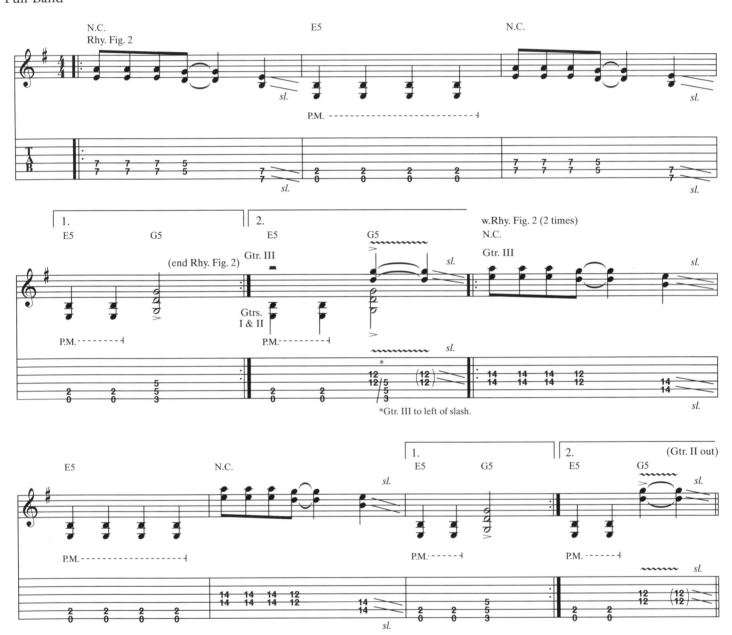

The Memory Remains

from *Reload*

Words and Music by
James Hetfield and Lars Ulrich

The intro riff and solo of this tune are both short, and will not take long to learn. The solo centers around dyads, and shows a way to expand your focus beyond single-note improvising.

Intro

Vocals in an instrumental intro? Yes . . . and with great results. Gtr. I locks in with the vocals, emphasizing the ♭VII– I (here, D5–E5) relationship and ending on an ominous ♭II, (here, F5). At the half time feel, the tuned-down E riff is played with a bottom-heavy distorted tone.

TRACK 36

Full Band

65

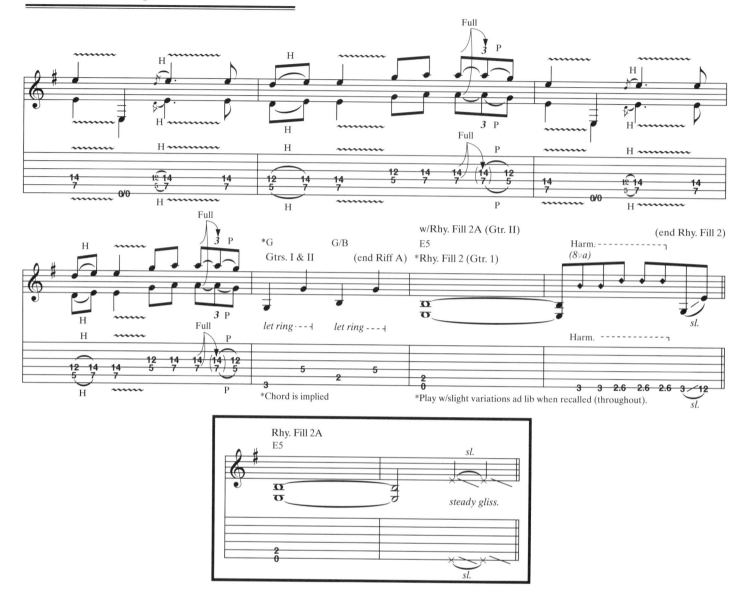

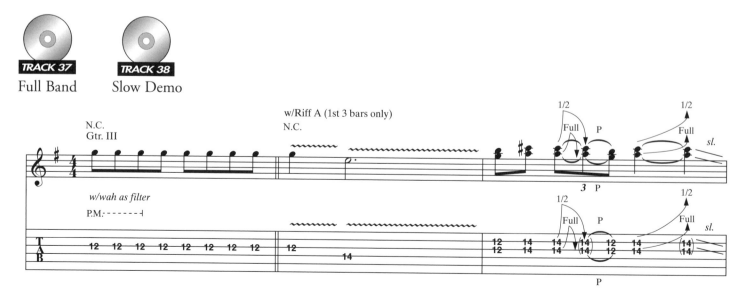

Solo

Preceded by unaccompanied, wah-inflected G's, Hammett whips out a series of soulful blues licks and bent dyads. Notice that, with the wah turned on, his tone is completely different than usual.

TRACK 37
Full Band

TRACK 38
Slow Demo

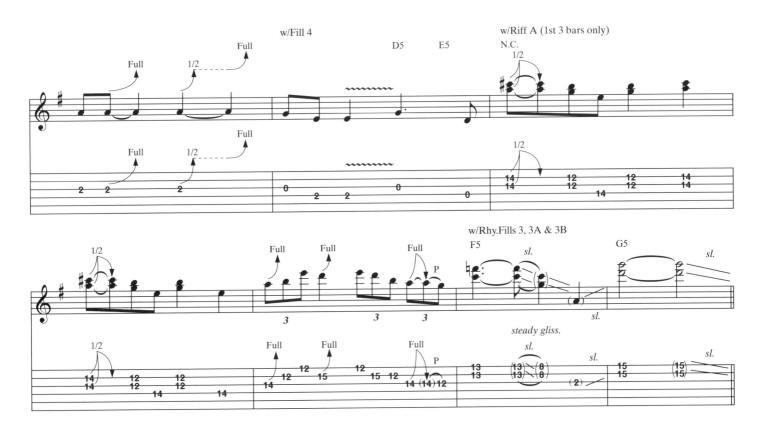

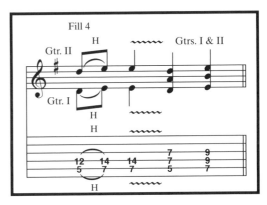

*Throughout song. Gtr. IV is processed through
a pitch shiting effect which causes notes
to sound an octave higher than written.

The Unforgiven II

from *Reload*

Words and Music by
James Hetfield, Lars Ulrich and Kirk Hammett

This new rendition of their original, "The Unforgiven," begins with distorted guitar before coming to the acoustic part that started the original version. (Trivia note: both versions are the fourth track on their respective albums.)

Intro

The opening distorted guitar yields a new melody, in octaves, over the original chord changes, and familiar sounds return with a pedal steel-style version of the "The Unforgiven" opening riff. These country-like bends are produced with a B-bender, but before you go out and install one, try using your fingers to bend the strings. (Note: the band is tuned down a half step for this version, which makes for easier bending).

Usually Metallica harmonizes in 3rds, 4ths, or 5ths, but Riff B brings forth two guitars harmonized in 6ths.

TRACK 39

Full Band

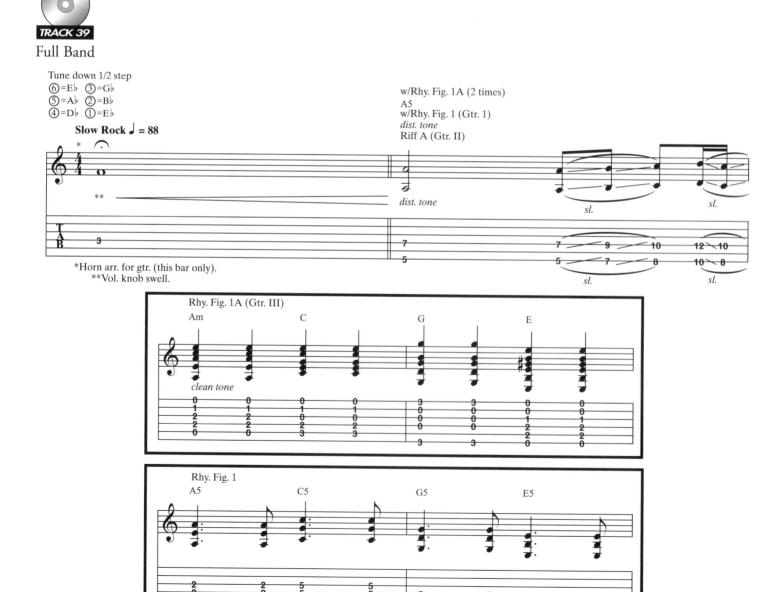

*Horn arr. for gtr. (this bar only).
**Vol. knob swell.

Solo

Hammett's return to a bluesier style can been heard in his solos throughout this album, with this solo being an obvious case in point! His drenching double-stop bends, classic blues licks, and '60s guitar tone make a convincing argument for his blues endeavors!

Dyads from the A Dorian mode are played in the first bar and in bars 6-8. Look for similar two-note fragments in your own study, and then work them into your improvisations.

TRACK 40
Full Band

TRACK 41
Slow Demo

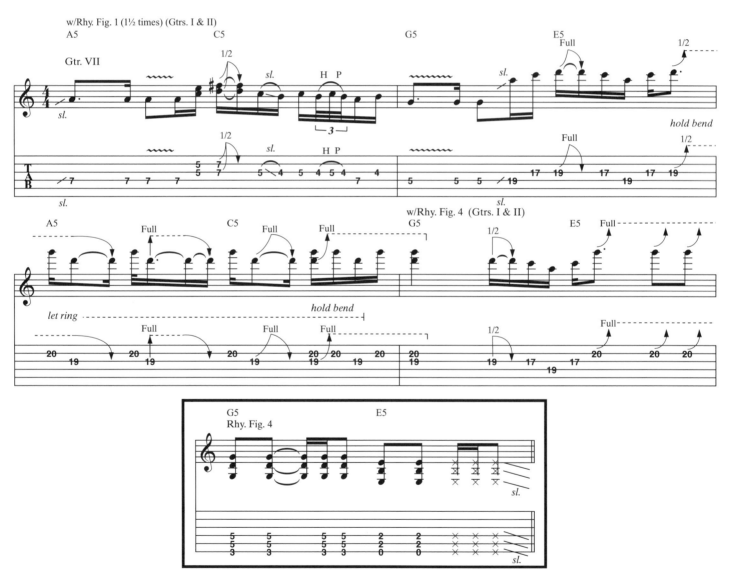

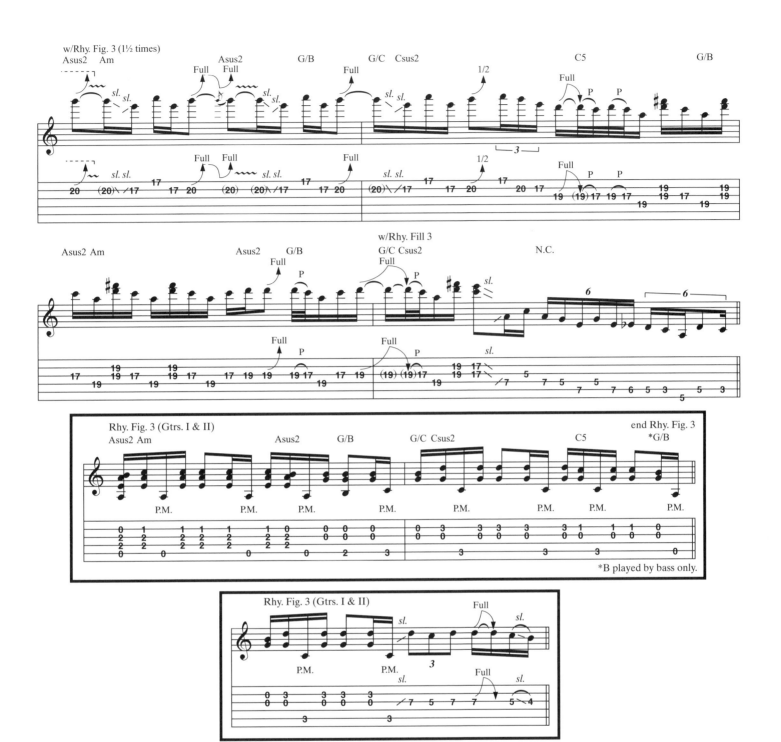

• Tablature Explanation/Notation Legend •

TABLATURE: A six-line staff that graphically represents the guitar fingerboard. By placing a number on the appropriate line, the string and the fret of any note can be indicated. For example:

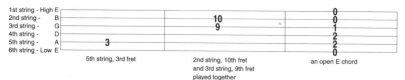

1st string - High E
2nd string - B
3rd string - G
4th string - D
5th string - A
6th string - Low E

5th string, 3rd fret   2nd string, 10th fret and 3rd string, 9th fret played together   an open E chord

Definitions for Special Guitar Notation

BEND: Strike the note and bend up a half step (one fret).

BEND: Strike the note and bend up a whole step (two frets).

BEND AND RELEASE: Strike the note and bend up a half (or whole) step, then release the bend back to the original note. All three notes are tied; only the first note is struck.

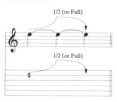

PRE-BEND: Bend the note up a half (or whole) step, then strike it.

PRE-BEND AND RELEASE: Bend the note up a half (or whole) step, strike it and release the bend back to the original note.

UNISON BEND: Strike the two notes simultaneously and bend the lower note to the pitch of the higher.

VIBRATO: Vibrate the note by rapidly bending and releasing the string with a left-hand finger.

WIDE OR EXAGGERATED VIBRATO: Vibrate the pitch to a greater degree with a left-hand finger or the tremolo bar.

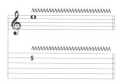

SLIDE: Strike the first note and then with the same left-hand finger move up the string to the second note. The second note is not struck.

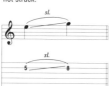

SLIDE: Same as above, except the second note is struck.

SLIDE: Slide up to the note indicated from a few frets below.

HAMMER-ON: Strike the first (lower) note, then sound the higher note with another finger by fretting it without picking.

PULL-OFF: Place both fingers on the notes to be sounded. Strike the first (higher) note, then sound the lower note by pulling the finger off the higher note while keeping the lower note fretted.

TRILL: Very rapidly alternate between the note indicated and the small note shown in parentheses by hammering on and pulling off.

TAPPING: Hammer ("tap") the fret indicated with the right-hand index or middle finger and pull off to the note fretted by the left hand.

NATURAL HARMONIC: With a left-hand finger, lightly touch the string over the fret indicated, then strike it. A chime-like sound is produced.

ARTIFICIAL HARMONIC: Fret the note normally and sound the harmonic by adding the right-hand thumb edge or index finger tip to the normal pick attack.

A.H. pitch: E

TREMOLO BAR: Drop the note by the number of steps indicated, then return to original pitch.

PALM MUTE: With the right hand, partially mute the note by lightly touching the string just before the bridge.

MUFFLED STRINGS: Lay the left hand across the strings without depressing them to the fretboard; strike the strings with the right hand, producing a percussive sound.

PICK SLIDE: Rub the pick edge down the length of the string to produce a scratchy sound.

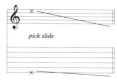

TREMOLO PICKING: Pick the note as rapidly and continuously as possible.

RHYTHM SLASHES: Strum chords in rhythm indicated. Use chord voicings found in the fingering diagrams at the top of the first page of the transcription.

SINGLE-NOTE RHYTHM SLASHES: The circled number above the note name indicates which string to play. When successive notes are played on the same string, only the fret numbers are given.